VoiceWorks

A "How-To" Owner's Manual
for Vocal Students and Teachers

by Henry A. Alviani

Basic High School Choir
400 Palo Verde Dr.
Henderson, NV 89015

Alfred

ACKNOWLEDGEMENT

Thanks to Julie Westlund of Mellen, WI,
and Debbie Henry of Clarion University for
their enormous assistance in helping to put
together the original and earlier versions of
this manuscript. Special thanks to my most
important proof-reader who represented the
primary target audience for this manual: my
then-15-year-old daughter, Rebekah.

alfred.com

Book (27465)
ISBN 10: 0-7390-4751-5
ISBN 13: 0-7390-4751-4

 # Contents

 # Foreword

I have spent the majority of my life juggling my interests and activities as an athlete (I played some college basketball and volleyball), a shade-tree mechanic (I still change my own oil and headlights and do many minor repairs), and a singer/musician. In my experience, I have found that the three have more similarities than differences. Many of these similarities have worked their way into my teaching style over the past twenty-five-plus years. In my effort to help students understand the mechanics and technique of vocal development, I frequently employ analogies that are designed to relate to other interests in their lives, such as sports and cars. This book is designed to share some of those analogies with you in the hope that it will help you in your efforts to better understand the vocal mechanism. You may want to find some of your own analogies and add them to the ones you find here; please feel free.

 # Chapter 1

Introduction

What do major professional sports hold during the off-season? I'm not talking about mini-camps or workouts or trades, but something where representatives from every team in the league gather together in one place at the same time to hold this annual event.

Give up?

They hold a draft.

The point of the draft is to acquire the rights to the most talented athletes that a team feels will meet their needs for the following year. A team may choose a player who is best at a particular position where they feel they are weakest, or sometimes they may pick the best athlete regardless of position. Once the draft is completed, each team then goes about the business of putting together the players into a unified force that is capable of accomplishing things as a unit that no individual would be capable of accomplishing alone. Arguably the best team consists of the best individual players functioning together under the guidance of the best coach. Certainly a team with less talented individual players but a better team concept is fully capable of beating a team with more talent but less unity as a team. On the other hand, a team with vastly superior individual talent may be able to defeat a less-talented team no matter how well it plays as a team. However, the goal is to combine the two—great individual talent and a superior team concept—into an unbeatable, unified force. The purpose of this manual is to help you develop your individual skills so that you can combine your talents with your singing "teammates" under your "coach's" leadership into a musical force that is capable of creating something that no individual is capable of creating alone.

Chapter 2

Posture

Why do choir directors always make such a big deal out of posture? Well, it's not for the same reason that a teacher in another class might have. It's not the same as, "Don't slouch, you look like a slob."

What's the Big Deal About Posture?

Think for a minute about how important posture is to an athlete. Only let's call it "form." Think about all the time baseball players spend studying their batting stance or pitching delivery, basketball players their shot, golfers their swing. Look at how many coaches there are on a pro team's staff. These are supposed to be the best players in the world, and yet it seems the higher the level, the more people they have helping them with their form.

Let's go a step further to sports that actually score the athletes on their posture. Take a second to list a few.

What did you come up with? Gymnastics? Diving? Ice-skating? Any others? So from an athlete's perspective, form or posture is not only critical to their success, it is the basis on which the winner of a competition is determined. Why is it any less important for a singer?

Let me ask you a question. What do you consider to be your "vocal instrument?" Take a minute to think or talk about this.

So what did you decide? My guess is some of you said your mouth, or your vocal cords, or your breath support system (more on that later!), or some other specific part of your body. Let's ask the same question about a piano. Is a piano the keys? The strings? The hammers? Are you starting to get the idea? **It's the whole instrument!**

Now what do you consider to be your "vocal instrument?" If you said your whole body, you got it. Posture is important because it affects your body's ability to function best as a singer. Suppose your instrument were a trumpet with dents, or a violin with a crack in the body, or a flute with a leaky pad. The form of the instrument is as critical to its proper function as your posture is to your ability as a singer.

What Makes Good Posture?

What is the best posture for singing? Try this little game. Stand with your feet slightly apart, about shoulder width, and go **completely limp** from the waist up. (That means your upper body will hang down as you bend at the waist.) Be sure your arms and your neck are as limp as cooked spaghetti. Now slowly start to straighten your back **from the waist,** building one vertebra on top of another, keeping your arms limp. The last part of your spine to straighten will be your neck. Are you straight? Let's find out. Reach into your pocket (if you don't have one, pretend) and pull out the eyehook that I secretly placed there. Screw the hook into the top of your head (still pretending). Now take the imaginary rope hanging from the hook in front of you and tie one end to the hook on top of your head. Toss the other end over the bar above and in front of you. Now grab the free end of the rope and give it a quick, firm tug. That should pull you up just a little bit straighter.

Now that your back and head are straight, you need to do one more thing. Remove the eyehook from the top of your head and screw it into your sternum (breastbone). Give the rope another tug. This will elevate your thorax (ribcage—I'll try to throw in a few technical terms every now and then). We'll discuss why this is important when we get to breathing. But for now just know that maintaining your thorax in an elevated position while you sing is important for two basic reasons. First, appearance. People watch you when you sing. A constant heaving up and down of the chest looks real cute on first graders, but it's very distracting when you're in junior or senior high school. Second, singing frequently requires taking large amounts of air in an incredibly brief amount of time. Big, quick breaths are quite common. If you allow the chest to collapse every time you sing, then you have to jerk the chest back up when you inhale. The muscular contraction required to pull up the chest can result in tension being transferred into the neck, which will affect the vocal mechanism. And you want to do everything you can to eliminate tension around the throat.

Now we're ready to talk about fueling your machine.

Chapter 3

Breathing

Your Voice is a Machine

Think of your voice as a machine. It has moving, working parts. It produces sound. Like any machine, it needs some kind of fuel to power it. The fuel source for your voice is air. Now I'm not going to tell you how to breathe. But I am going to talk with you about how to breathe in a way that will make you a better, more effective singer and will make the singing experience more enjoyable for both you and for anyone who listens to you. And that's the whole point of singing, isn't it?

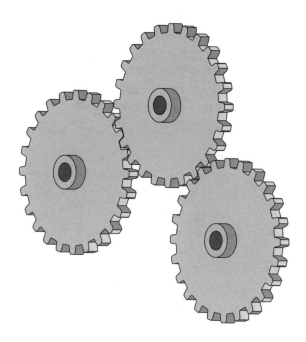

If you've ever noticed the publicity that precedes a boxing match, you may have seen what was referred to in my local paper when I was a kid as "The Tale of the Tape." The two boxers get measured every way imaginable: height, weight, length of their reach, how big their biceps, thighs, calves, fists, and neck are. There is also a measurement that really isn't technically accurate. It's "chest normal" and "chest expanded." The problem with this measurement is that the chest doesn't really expand. As you found out in Chapter 2, it elevates. Think about it. Your ribs are all connected to the spine in the back, and until you get near the bottom of the thorax, they're all connected to the sternum, the xiphoid cartilage (just below the sternum), and the costal cartilage in the front. The chest can't expand. The ribs are fixed front and back. However, they are hinged at the spine, which allows the chest muscles to pull the thorax upward to create more room for the lungs to expand. Remember the eyehook in the sternum? This is why you need to keep the thorax elevated all the time when you sing.

The Mechanics of Breathing to Power Your Voice

There are two very separate and important elements to breathing, and a good singer learns both to master them individually and coordinate them. One is inhaling, or *inspiration*. The other is exhaling, or *expiration*. Think of your voice production the way you think of the mechanics of a car in the simplest terms. You need fuel, you need to put the car in gear, you need to take the emergency brake off, and you need someone to direct and control the car. This chapter is about the fuel part.

I'm going to try to bust a few myths along the way. The first one is the classic line, "Support with your diaphragm." Even Buffy the Vampire Slayer used the phrase in her TV show regarding the proper and most effective way to scream, and if you can't believe Buffy, whom can you believe? The reality is, the diaphragm is a muscle of inspiration. When relaxed, it sits across the middle of your body in a domed shape, forming the floor of your *thoracic cavity* (ribcage) and the ceiling of your *abdominal cavity* (belly). When you inhale, the diaphragm contracts and flattens out. This action in effect creates a bit of a vacuum inside your thorax, and air goes in through the mouth and nose to fill up the vacuum and equalize the air pressure. (Sorry, Buffy.)

This is the same way you drink through a straw. When you suck on a straw, what you're actually doing is creating a vacuum inside your mouth. (That's why your cheeks collapse. Just for the fun of it, try sucking in your cheeks with your mouth open. You can't do it.) Since the air pressure *outside* your mouth is greater than the air pressure *inside* your mouth and is constantly pushing down on whatever you're drinking, the greater air pressure pushes the liquid up through the straw and into your mouth.

First, Inspiration

One of our objectives is to learn how to tank up with as much air as is necessary, which sometimes can be quite a large order. Try this. Sit down on the front edge of your seat; place your hands on your waist (right hand on right side, left hand on left side—you'd be amazed how many people get confused by this direction!), with the thumbs in front and the fingers in back. Bend forward as far as you can with your head towards your knees. Now take as big a breath as you can. You should be able to feel an expansion in your lower back where your fingers are. As soon as you feel this, stand up (remember to keep your vertebrae aligned and your chest elevated). Leaving your hands on your waist, inhale and try to feel the expansion you felt when you were sitting down. It won't be nearly as obvious, but you should feel something. This is the place where you want to focus your attention when you inhale while singing. If you do this regularly, habitually, you will develop the ability to increase your breath capacity.

Now, Let's Work on Expiration

Take in a full tank of air, concentrating on expanding in the back. Now hiss as hard as you can, pushing not from the abdominal area, but from the back. The funny thing is if you focus on supporting from the back, **you don't have to worry about supporting from the front.** It's automatic. As a matter of fact, supporting from the back *increases* the level of support in the front. This is the "gas pedal" of your vocal mechanism.

Let's test this. Pair off, preferably with someone your own height, and follow this exercise step-by-step. Facing each other, place your left hand on top of your partner's right shoulder. **Gently** place your right fist in your partner's stomach just above the beltline. Turn your faces turned toward the front of the room, to prevent you both from spraying into each other's faces. Now you're going to do four things simultaneously:

1. Pull your partner toward you with your left hand;

2. Push your partner away from you with your right hand;

3. Keep your back perfectly straight to prevent you from folding in half;

4. Support from the back and hiss as hard as you can.

Be sure you start at the same time. Do this two or three times. Don't go easy on your partners. Make them work hard to resist the pressure you're applying to their abdominal area. This will give you an idea of the constant level of support a good singer needs. You need to think conscientiously about supporting with this level of intensity. After awhile, it will become habitual and you won't be able to remember what it was like to sing with inadequate support.

Now let's apply this breathing technique to the production of sound. Face forward, hands on your waist (to remind you to support from the back), and on the signal your director gives you, take a full breath and hiss as hard as you can. Now let's go a step further. In a three-count rhythm,

1. Inhale,

2. hiss, and,

3. with the same level of intensity as when you are hissing, open up from a hiss to the vowel "aw."

Actually, with the hiss, it will come out "sa-a-a-a-a-aw." This is the part about taking off the emergency brake. You should feel absolutely no restriction in the throat when producing this sound.

Releasing Tension in the Vocal Mechanism—Using the "Legs" of Your Voice

If you've ever lifted a heavy box, you know the proper technique is to bend the knees so you can take the strain off your back. When you get to be my age, protecting your back becomes a very important concern. Treating your voice the same way is critical to your vocal health. Singing well, with power and expression, requires a certain amount of physical intensity. Instinctively you already know this to be true. In the same way that your car works best when the gas pedal is pressed and the emergency brake is off, your voice works best when you use adequate breath support and eliminate restriction in the throat. The more intensity you use to provide that breath support, the more tension you can eliminate.

Here's another way to think about releasing tension around the throat. In Southern California, kelp, or seaweed, can grow up to a foot a day. If you've ever seen it, you know it feels like rubber and is very flexible. It must be in order to sway with the currents in which it lives and grows. Pretend you are kelp. Anchor your feet to the floor and sway as if you are kelp in the ocean current. Especially keep your neck very loose and flexible. While you're doing this, start to sing. Notice if your neck remains loose and flexible or becomes stiff and tense. If it tenses, keep trying this until you can eliminate the tension and sing without restriction.

Another way to think about the relationship between breath support and the vocal mechanism is to think about how important legs are to an athlete's performance. Anyone play basketball? Take a five-foot jump shot. Think about how much power from the legs is involved. Then back up to the free-throw line. Then to the three-point arc. If you shoot correctly, your arm and hand technique should not significantly change at all. So where do you get the extra power necessary for a longer shot? It must come from somewhere.

From the legs, of course.

The arm and hand are for control and finesse. If you add power and strength to the arm as you get farther from the basket, you sacrifice that control. Think about all your basic positions in volleyball. Passing, setting, blocking, hitting, digging all require you to start from a bent-knee position to be most effective, so that you can use the power of your legs to perform all of those skills properly. What is the source of power when you're tackling, blocking, or running through the line in football? How about batting? Pushing off the mound when you pitch? It's the legs that give you the power you need.

Your breathe support is the "legs" of your vocal production.

You need to develop a habit of supporting your tone throughout your range regardless of where you are singing. However, you will probably learn that as you ascend into the higher portion of your range, you will require even more physical intensity to support the tone. The vocal cords are stretching more tightly in order to vibrate faster and produce the higher pitches. Imagine you're riding a bike or driving a car on level ground, and you see a hill coming up. You want to maintain the same speed. Obviously it will require more power, either from your legs if you're on a bike, or more gas if you're in a car. Just be careful not to relax when you get to a more comfortable part of your range. You know what happens to a team that gets up for the tougher opponents but lets down its intensity when it plays the league doormat. It needs to play every team with the same intensity that is the result of a habit that is developed from practicing with intensity.

Developing High Quality "Raw Material"

Now, granted, I wouldn't buy a ticket to come hear you produce that huge "aw" sound. But it is great "raw material" for building a great vocal tone. Anyone seen Michelangelo's statue David? Or at least seen a picture of it? Michelangelo sculpted it from 1501 to 1503. My question to you is: what do you suppose it looked like in 1500? A big chunk of white rock. Actually, it was a twenty-foot-high piece of Carrara marble, which he considered to be the world's finest carving marble. In other words, it was the best in raw material he could find. He would travel to Carrara to visit the quarry and select his own marble for sculpting. It was then a matter of him applying his genius and skill to create one of the world's great works of art that today stands in a museum in Florence, Italy, for anyone to see and enjoy.

You need to think of your voice as great raw material that you can "sculpt" to create great musical art.

Chapter 4

The Vocal Cords

Here are a few interesting (at least to me) items about the vocal cords (not chords).

The vocal cords are located inside your larynx, protected by the *thyroid cartilage* or "Adam's apple." They are actually ligaments controlled by muscles that surround them, making them longer or shorter, thinner or thicker, depending on the signal your brain sends to them in order to produce the pitch you want to sing. You don't have any actual control over the cords. Through a complicated process that's way beyond me, you think the pitch with what I like to call your "inner ear." That message is sent from your brain to the cords, and the adjustment in the length and thickness of the cords happens instantly to produce the correct pitch. The cords are connected together in front to the inside of the thyroid cartilage and at the back to two little cartilage called *corniculates*. These sit on top of two sort of pyramid-shaped cartilage called arytenoids, which are pretty amazing little things. They can slide open to allow you to breathe by creating a space between the cords called the *glottis*. They slide together to bring the cords next to each other, or *approximate,* so that air can pass through the tiny opening between them, causing them to vibrate and create sound. And they can snug tightly against each other, causing the cords to cut off the flow of air by sealing the *trachea,* or windpipe, which is how you hold your breath.

What Do the Vocal Cords Do?

The most important function of your vocal cords, surprisingly, is **not** making sound. Actually, that's way down the list of things the cords are responsible for doing. Their primary purpose is to protect the lungs from letting anything other than air pass through them. That's why you cough when you accidentally inhale the smallest amount of liquid. Also why people who smoke coughed when they first started, and most still do on occasion now. Smoke obviously is a foreign substance that does not belong in the lungs, and the vocal cords know this. That's why they try to keep out smoke by coughing. **So don't smoke!** But you already knew that. Enough said.

Another important function of the vocal cords is to help you lift heavy objects. Excuse me?! Think about it. Usually, when you lift something heavy, don't you hold your breath? You may let out a little grunt, but that's just a bit of air escaping between the cords that otherwise are fully closed, or *approximated*. Without that air pressure trapped inside your lungs, the chest muscles have no leverage except against the ribs. You've probably seen enough medical dramas to know that when paramedics or ER doctors are pushing on someone's chest to get the heart going again, they sometimes crack ribs. Theoretically (but not very likely), someone could be strong enough that if they contracted their chest muscles without compressed air inside to stabilize the thorax, they could crush their own ribs.

The Power of Air Pressure—and the Power of the Vocal Cords to Resist It

What's the point of this little digression? First of all, think about how powerful the force of air pressure can be. What does your car actually ride on? Compressed air, held in the shape of the tire that contains it. Remove the air (lower the air pressure) and you go nowhere. What stops a semi? Air brakes. Think about all the air pressure you produced with the hissing exercise. Now think about how powerful your vocal cords must be to withstand all that pressure inside your lungs. Your cords are controlled by very powerful little muscles, so they can sustain a great deal of pressure. In fact, they require air pressure to function properly.

Here's a small illustration from your history book. Do you remember the great contribution the ancient Romans made to architecture? It was the Roman arch. What made it so important is that it replaced the old Greek method of post-and-lintel (take a look at all of your doorframes—that's post-and-lintel

design). The problem with the post-and-lintel design was that the more weight you piled on top, the more likely it was to collapse under the stress. Just the opposite was true with the Roman arch. The more weight you placed on the keystone at the top of the arch, the stronger the columns became. Your vocal cords are like that. Here's a little demonstration.

Pair up again. Stand face-to-face with your partner and put up both of your hands in front of you about shoulder height against your partner's hands. One of you will play the part of the vocal cords, the other will be air pressure. When the one who is air pressure applies no pressure to the one who is the vocal cords, the "cord-person" naturally will respond with no pressure. But as the "breath-person" increases the pressure, the "cord-person" responds with an equal amount of pressure to keep from being pushed over. This is how your vocal cords work. They are capable of withstanding a tremendous amount of air pressure.

By developing the proper breathing technique, you can actually increase the power with which the cords can withstand the air pressure being exerted on them. As a matter of fact, the vocal cord muscles will build muscle mass through exercise as you develop your breathing technique. This will allow you to sing with greater power, control, and flexibility. On the other hand, singers who are used to singing daily in rehearsals during the school year and then don't sing at all during the summer will find that they may lose some of the power and control they developed because the muscles controlling the vocal cords actually atrophy and lose muscle mass. Fortunately, this is easily resolved by getting back into a regular routine of singing. Better yet, find some place to continue singing during the summer so you don't lose that muscle tone. If you're an athlete and want to continue to improve, more than likely you continue to play ball or lift weights or do something else to continue your development during the off-season. And if you like to sing, why not do the same thing?

Things That May or May Not Affect Your Vocal Cords

It's time for another myth-buster. You've probably heard a million stories about what not to eat or drink before singing, or what to drink that will help your vocal cords. The reality is **nothing you eat or drink has any immediate, direct effect on your vocal cords.** Think about it. Your vocal cords are located at the top of your trachea. The trachea is for one thing only—air. The most common myth is that milk "coats your throat." But anything you ingest goes down the esophagus, bypassing the trachea. That's why the larynx ascends and the epiglottis drops down to cover the trachea like a sealed lid when you swallow. It is true that if you have an intolerance to lactose, drinking milk may have an impact on your vocal cords, but it's a much longer, more involved process than simply drinking a glass of milk. Briefly, here's how it works. Lactose is counteracted in your digestive system by an enzyme called lactase.

Some people don't have enough lactase in their system and as a result are lactose-intolerant. When you reach this point where there is more lactose than your system can handle (I suppose everyone could reach that point sometime), a second "line of defense" kicks in—*histamine*. You've all heard of over-the-counter cold or allergy remedies that have an antihistamine. Histamine is released generally throughout your system through the mucous membranes. You have these membranes in your sinus area, which keep your nasal passages moist, but also is why your head gets all stuffed up when you have a cold or allergies. You also have mucous membranes in your larynx. These are vital to lubricate your vocal cords. Imagine trying to play a clarinet or saxophone with a dry reed. That squawking sound it would make is what your voice would be like without mucous to lubricate your cords. But too much mucous will cause you to clear your throat constantly. If that happens, the very best thing you can do for yourself is drink plenty of water to help thin the mucous and clear out the excess.

Some people can drink a gallon of milk or eat a half-gallon of ice cream before singing with no adverse effect, while others may be so lactose-intolerant that they get gummed up just driving past a cow. It's entirely an individual thing. But the main point is that you cannot eat or drink anything that will go directly to your vocal cords and "coat your throat."

There are also many stories about what you can drink to clear up your cords. Some of the more popular myths include lemon juice, hot tea with lemon, carrot juice, or even a glass of wine. (By the way, alcohol can do nothing but interfere with your muscular control over the vocal cords, just like an athlete, as well as affect your mental alertness and dry you out. So drinking alcohol before you sing is **never** a good idea, even when you're old enough to drink legally. Caffeine is also a bad idea since it dries you out.) Again, **nothing you eat or drink has any immediate, direct effect on your vocal cords.** Now, having said that, if you find that, with the exception of alcohol or caffeine, something you drink before singing makes you feel better and you believe you sing better after drinking it, then by all means go ahead and drink it. The mental aspect of singing, like athletics, is just as critical to your success as the physical.

What About Coughing or Clearing My Throat?

A word of caution. Coughing, or even clearing your throat harshly or excessively, can be very abusive to your vocal cords. You may have had an opportunity to see a cough on film. If you have, then you know it's a very violent thing. If you're at all concerned about the health of your vocal cords, learn to be very gentle when you feel the need to cough or clear your throat. Obviously, there are times when coughing is necessary. But I have found that many people clear their throats out of habit, for no real reason, and excessive coughing can cause irritation that will only make you want to cough more, which will cause more irritation, which will make you want to cough more, which will...you get the point. If you are dealing with a cold that has you coughing a lot without any real benefit, find a good remedy that includes a cough suppressant. And if you clear your throat out of habit, find a better habit to replace it.

—

Chapter 5

Tone

For me, the single most important quality that distinguishes a trained, rehearsed choral group from a "congregational" sound is the group's tone quality. Basically, tone is the way you sing your vowels (we'll look at consonants later). As a matter of fact, there are many wonderful pieces that do not use words at all, but just the beauty of the human vocal tone. Listen to the last movement of Gustav Holst's *The Planets*, one of the best-known examples of singing without words.

Resonance and How It Affects Vocal Tone

The challenge for the singer is to find a way to create the most beautiful, resonant tone possible. The best way to do this is to maximize your resonating space. Basically, there are four of these spaces. Three of them are located in the passage that goes from your vocal cords to the area behind your nose, called the *pharynx* (pronounced "FARE-inks). They are the *laryngeal pharynx*, the space immediately above the *larynx* (pronounced "LAIR-inks"), or voice-box, where the vocal cords are, the *oropharynx*, the space immediately behind the mouth, where your tonsils are, and the *nasopharynx*, the space behind the nose. The fourth resonating chamber is the *oral cavity* or mouth. Let's deal with each of these areas one at a time.

The biggest problem with the laryngeal pharynx is the darned thing keeps wanting to slide up. It's supposed to when you swallow, in order to protect your lungs, but it can cause a problem when you sing. Find your *thyroid cartilage* or "Adam's apple." It's usually a bit easier to find on men than women because it tends to be larger and more obvious, and usually easier on altos than sopranos and on basses than tenors for the same reason. To make sure you know where it is, touch it with your fingertips, then swallow. It should slide up as the *epiglottis* (a tongue-shaped piece of cartilage at the top of the trachea, or windpipe) drops down to seal off the trachea. This action prevents anything you swallow from "going down the wrong pipe" and causing you to choke. Now yawn. The thyroid cartilage will probably drop down, creating more space in the laryngeal pharynx, which is why yawns sound so hollow or "yawny."

Now sing an octave scale, keeping your finger on your thyroid cartilage. It *should* stay almost perfectly still. More than likely, however, it probably slid up as you ascended the scale. Think about what this does to your resonance. As the thyroid cartilage rises, it reduces the amount of resonating space in the laryngeal pharynx by making it smaller. If this is your problem (and it is for most people), try doing two things that may help you control it. First, think "yawn" when you sing. This will help make you conscious of the position of the thyroid cartilage. Second, keep a finger on your thyroid cartilage every second you possibly can while singing to remind yourself to keep it in that neutral position. Keep doing this until it stays put habitually. It may take awhile. Be patient with yourself. It took me a year-and-a-half.

One warning. If you think about yawning while you sing, be careful to use only the "top half" of the yawn, the part that will help you create as much space as possible in the oropharynx and oral cavity. You don't want the thyroid cartilage to drop down too far (the "bottom half" of the yawn) or you'll end up with that hollow "yawny" sound.

The oropharynx and oral cavity are a bit easier to deal with. The best thing you can do is to think about creating all of your vowels as vertically as possible, or about using the "top half" of a yawn, like I just mentioned. We'll get into this a lot more when we talk about vowel formation.

Singing With a Nasal Tone Quality

The nasopharynx is the least important of the four resonating chambers. As a matter of fact, if you use the nasopharynx too much, you end up with a very nasal sound because too much sound is coming through the nose. This tone is fine for some styles of music, like country. As a matter of fact, it's essential in order to get the right character of country singing. But you want to develop the ability to control the tone any way you want. It's like being able to choose either to go to the hoop or pull up for the jumper, or to go with the pitch to hit into any field. There are many examples in sports that demonstrate how important it is to be able to learn to master a variety of techniques so you can be flexible enough to go with what works best in any situation.

Here are a couple of good ways to find out if you're singing with too much nasal quality. As you're singing, gently touch your nose with your finger and thumb on either side. If you feel a lot of vibration, that's an indication that a lot of the sound is going through the nose. Another way is to gently squeeze the nose closed, then open, and continue back and forth while you're holding out a sustained note. If the tone changes, it means some of the sound is coming out through the nose. The greater the change in tone, the more sound is coming through the nose. When sound comes through the nose it will naturally have a nasal quality. It will also muffle the tone and reduce your volume. Since dynamics are one of the important techniques singers use to be expressive, this muffling will limit your ability to create the type of dynamic range that will help make you a more expressive singer. Try to focus the sound through the mouth to get the richest, most resonant tone you can.

Focus as Part of Good Tone and Projection

Another critical aspect of tone is its focus. Up until some years ago, radios and televisions had to be tuned in by hand using a tuning knob. You would find the station you wanted, but if the tuning dial was a little bit off, a slight adjustment was necessary to clear up the signal and bring the station into clear focus. Most voices are a lot like that. Your goal is to develop the clearest, most focused singing tone possible, eliminating any suggestion of breathiness.

The most common hindrance to a clear, focused tone is breathiness. Resolving this problem, just like in any athletic skill, requires a combination of physical and mental attention. Physically, breath support is the most important, key element to achieving good tonal focus (remember the Roman arch). Mentally, think of your voice as being like a garden hose with an adjustable nozzle. You can create a very gentle, widespread spray, like what you would use to water a newly planted bed of very delicate flowers. You can adjust the nozzle to create a full, easy flow that you would use to fill a pail with water. Or you could go a step further and create a jet stream that is capable of cleaning the windows on the second floor of a house. Or think of your voice as a flashlight. Start with the cheap kind that casts a soft, wide glow on an area but doesn't really light up anything. Imagine if you could adjust a nozzle on that flashlight and turn it into one of those big, police-issue jobs that takes four "D" batteries and shoots a beam like a searchlight.

Now take it a step further and concentrate that energy into a laser beam that has the power to cut metal. The laser beam and the second-floor window washer analogies are examples of the ability you want your voice to develop. This results in what people refer to as projection.

Find a spot on a wall, preferably something round, or have someone hold up something small and round, about the size of a thumb and finger making a circle. Or just have someone hold up a thumb and finger in a circle. Visually and mentally focus on that circle. Choose whether you want your voice to be a garden hose or a flashlight. Now sing the vowel "oo" through that circle without letting any "water" or "light" touch that circle. Try it again with other vowels, then with a phrase or a whole song. This will help you practice to mentally focus your voice.

There are many benefits that come from developing a more focused tone. Your voice will carry farther (projection). You will have a greater dynamic range, giving you more ability to use dynamics as a means of expression and interpretation. Because you are using less air to produce sound by eliminating breathiness, you will be able to carry phrases longer. It's very much like a car that has just been given a tune-up. The car is able to go farther, with more power, on less gas.

A word of caution about the term *projection*. Projection is not something you do; it is the **result** of something you do. In the relationship of cause-and-effect, the cause is posture, breath support, elimination of tension around the throat, good tonal concept, and mental focus. The effect (or result) is projection. Do not ever try to project. Do the other things correctly, and as a consequence you will project. I say this because I have had too many voice students who sang with well-intentioned but poorly informed directors who kept demanding the singers to project without ever explaining to them how. Their result was tremendous strain on the voice and a world of vocal problems that took months to resolve. Their effort was never in question, just their method of going about achieving what they thought was projection. I never tell students to project. If they do the other things correctly, projection will come.

Vocal Registers and the Passaggio—the "Gears" of Your Voice

Finally, you may have heard a discussion at some point about terms like "head voice," "chest voice," and *passaggio*. The first two terms are really more myths than anything else. We all use the terms, and we think we have an idea of what they mean. But in reality they have no meaning. The myth is that somehow these are the places where your voice resonates: in the head for higher notes, in the chest for lower notes. Let's think about this logically for a moment. All singing sound is the result of air passing between the vocal cords, causing them to vibrate. The air continues upward until it exits through the mouth. It **can't** go backward into the chest. The main resonating chambers are in the throat area *above* the larynx and in the mouth, with only minor (if any) resonation occurring in the nasal area. There is no room for any resonating space in the chest or in the head. You may feel that there is some vibration in the chest or in the head when you sing, but this is nothing more than what we call *sympathetic vibration*. It is not resonation.

However, you do have at least two major *registers* or "gears" in your vocal range. Think of them as you would the gears in an automatic transmission that shift smoothly as you pick up RPMs (more on this later). These gears are more correctly referred to as *lower register* and *upper register*. (Some believe there may actually be many more minor shifts, perhaps as many as one for each note in your range, but for now we only need to consider this one major shift.) Most of us speak in the lower register. Consequently, the upper register is usually underdeveloped because it doesn't receive anywhere near the amount of use the lower register does, and that's why so many new singers are more comfortable singing in the lower register.

You Have Two Major, Simultaneous Goals

First, develop both registers throughout your range so that they are equal in strength and ability. After all, most music is written without regard to whether or not it fits comfortably into someone's lower or upper register. A good basketball player learns to do many things with either hand: dribble, pass, shoot lay-ups. A tennis player learns to develop both a good forehand and backhand with equal power and skill. Some baseball players learn to switch-hit, and others become equally good at bunting or swinging for the cheap seats. A successful golfer needs to be equally good at driving and putting. Regardless of what voice part you consider yourself to be, it's better for you to develop all of your range. Furthermore, you'll want to concentrate on the part of your voice that is weakest, just like you'd spend more time practicing your backhand if it were weaker or less accurate than your forehand.

Second, you want to develop the ability to move easily and comfortably from one register to the other in the course of a song. Remember the analogy of the operation of a car in its simplest terms. You put the car in gear (drive, in an automatic), release the emergency brake (eliminate tension in the throat), step on the gas (breath support), and steer (mental focus and tonal concept). Your larynx is the gearbox or transmission. Remember it's an automatic. If you concentrate on the three essential elements of good vocal production— good focus and tonal concept, solid breath support, and release of tension in the throat—then you will learn to shift smoothly and effortlessly from one gear (register) to the other and back, just like in a car with a properly functioning automatic transmission.

 Some singers attempt to control the shifting from one register to the other as if it were a manual or stick transmission. You wouldn't try that with an automatic. Don't try it with your voice. Memorize this question:

What is the best possible tone I can produce on any given pitch?

If you can answer this question on a note-by-note basis, as fast as they go flying by, you've come a long way toward becoming a singer with a consistently good tone.

Now, having explained how this works, the best advice is to forget everything you just read, step on the gas, get out of the way, and let the larynx do its job.

Chapter 6

Vowels

Music is sung on the vowels. The key to creating the best, most consistently beautiful vocal tone is to sing all vowels vertically. Some vowels are easier to sing vertically than others, so some will naturally be more of a challenge than others. I want to concentrate on just eight vowel sounds. If you can master these eight and learn how to combine them into *diphthongs,* you will have gone a long way toward developing a tone that is consistently beautiful.

Some of you may be familiar with the International Phonetic Alphabet (IPA). While I have nothing against it (and for those of you who are serious about vocal training past high school, it would be very helpful to learn it and how it applies to your singing technique), I feel for our purposes it's a bit of overkill. So let's concentrate just on these eight. Five of them are the ones you commonly find in foreign languages like Italian, Spanish, and Latin. (German and French have a few other sounds with which we won't concern ourselves right now.) They are what we refer to as "pure vowels," and basically every time you see that vowel, it's pronounced the same way:

The vowel "a" is pronounced "ah" as in "father"

The vowel "e" is pronounced "eh" as in "bed"

The vowel "i" is pronounced "ee" as in "need"

The vowel "o" is pronounced "oh" as in "boat"

The vowel "u" is pronounced "oo" as in "food"

Ah—eh—ee—oh—oo.

Many of you have probably gone through this routine in a foreign language class. But now we're going a step farther to talk about the best way to pronounce these vowels as they apply to classical singing tone.

How to Form Vertical Vowels

There are any number of ways any vowel can be pronounced. What we're trying to achieve is a consistency of "tone color." Ever gone to a paint store to buy a can of white paint? One time I counted 24 different shades of white! Think of the five vowels as five different colors, say, red, yellow, green, blue, and purple. How many different shades of blue can you name, from sky blue to navy blue? How many examples can you find in this room? They all may be blue, but nobody would say they all are exactly the same blue. The difference is in the color's tone, the same term we use to describe the difference from one "ah" to another, or one "ee" to another. The five colors listed here might all be pastels, or metallic, or neon. We can say the same thing about vocal tone color. In fact voice teachers talk about and use the term tone color all the time. A trained classical tone color would be like fire engine red, canary yellow, forest green, royal blue, and the purple on the Los Angeles Lakers jerseys. Deep, rich, vibrant tones.

Let's start with the easiest vowel to form vertically, "ah." Loose jaw; be sure the tongue lays comfortably on the bottom of the mouth, not curled back, its tip just behind the bottom teeth. Sing that vowel, remembering everything you've learned about posture, breath support, and tone production. It will be helpful later on if you're in the habit of gently placing your hands on either side of your face to remind you to keep the vowels formed vertically, so do that now.

Now, without changing the shape of the outside of your mouth, say the vowel "eh." You will notice there is a change in the position of the tongue, but the position of the mouth and jaw should remain unchanged. Gently placing our hands on the side of your face will help remind you of this.

Go back to "ah." Concentrate on the vertical space you've created in the oropharynx and oral cavity. Keep that space right where it is, point the lips (pucker), and say the vowel "ooh." The difficulty with the "ooh" vowel is that when you close the lips to form it, there also is a tendency to shut down the back of the mouth which causes a loss of resonating space. Be sure to keep that space vertical and open.

Now comes the most difficult of the five vowels to keep resonant: the "ee" vowel. Keep your lips forward and the back of the mouth vertical and open as in the "oo" vowel. This is the same vertical position you use for "ee." Just for the fun of it, say "ee" with a horizontal placement. Go back and forth a few times between the two ways of saying "ee" and the difference between the two will be very obvious.

There are three more vowels that pose a particular problem in English that are not found as commonly in other languages. They are the short "a," "i," and "u." Think of the vowels in the words cat, kit, and cut, or lack, lick, and luck. Simply put, the best thing you can do to help you create these vowels with a dark, rich tone color that is consistent with the colors of the five "pure" vowels is to form them just as vertically. If you can master a consistently vertical production of these eight vowel sounds, you've got most of what you need to know about vowel production covered.

Hopefully you haven't gotten the idea that I'm saying there is only one correct tone for all types of music. Quite the opposite is true. Each different type of music—opera, musical theatre, country, rock, whatever— requires a certain tone that is appropriate. That's called style. But the reality is if you can learn to sing with the richest, most resonant tone color you're capable of producing, you can always go back and lighten or otherwise alter it to produce the stylistically appropriate tone. Think about colors of paint. If you start with a dark, rich color, you can always lighten it by adding white. But once you've lightened it, you can never get it back to its original darker tone. It's always easier to lighten the tone once you've learned to produce a darker, richer tone than the other way around. So learn to sing with the best, richest, darkest, most "classical" tone you can. You can always adjust it to sing other styles of music, and it will actually improve your ability to sing them.

Diphthongs—Like Salt on Eggs

English is filled with combinations of vowels sounds. When two vowel sounds are combined into a single syllable, these are called diphthongs, and when three are combined into a single syllable, triphthongs. In each case, one of the vowel sounds, called the sustaining vowel, is held out for virtually the entire length of the note. The other vowel or vowel sounds, called vanishing vowels, are barely voiced at all, but are essential to making the syllable sound complete and correct. This practice sheet will help you learn the best way to sing these special vowel combinations.

Diphthong Practice Sheet

Take a piece of paper and cover the right side of the chart on the next page. On the left side, mark all sustaining vowels with a short horizontal line above the group of letters and all vanishing vowels with a short curved line above the group of letters. There is no need to mark the consonants. Then check on the right side to see if you correctly identified the word that the sounds represent. Form all vowels vertically (a = ah, e = eh, i = ee, o = oh, u = oo) as in typical Italian or Latin pronunciation. Here's an example to get you started: d + eh + ee = day. The vowel sound "eh" is the sustaining vowel, so you would draw a short horizontal line above it. The vowel sound "ee" is the vanishing vowel, so you would draw a short curved line above it. Try saying the word "day," holding out the "eh" vowel for three full seconds before resolving to the "ee" vowel. Now try to do the rest of the practice sheet.

PRACTICE SHEET

b + oh + ee	boy
n + ah + oo	now
s + eh + ee	say
fl + ah + ee	fly
f + ee + oo	few
ee + oh + k	yoke
bl + oh + oo	blow
ah + oo + t	out
oo + eh + t	wet
ee + ah + n	yawn
oo + ee + d	weed
ee + eh + t	yet
f + eh + ee + th	faith
n + ah + ee + t	night
ee + ah + oo	yow
oo + ah + oo	wow
oo + eh + ee	way
oo + ah + ee	why

You may notice some consistent characteristics about the words on this list. The two most common diphthongs seem to be the long "a" and the long "i." The long "a" is always pronounced "eh + ee," never "ay." The long "i" is always pronounced "ah + ee." Also, you may have noticed that every word that begins with a "y" starts with an "ee" sound, and every word that begins with a "w" starts with an "oo" sound. Some conductors may prefer to have you pronounce words that begin with "wh" by switching the first two letters and putting the "h" before the "w" (or phonetically, the "oo"): why becomes hoo + ah + ee.

In pronouncing a syllable with a diphthong, the relationship of the sustaining vowel to the vanishing vowel is like the proportion of ingredients in a recipe. Take something very simple: fried eggs. Let's say you like a little salt on your eggs and nothing else. You have two ingredients: eggs and salt. What's the proportion? Let's say it's 100:1. Just enough salt to flavor the eggs to your liking, but not so much that it tastes salty. You might think so little salt compared to the amount of egg has no effect. But if you do like salt on your eggs, you'd probably still notice if it was missing. Look at the example of the word "few." Until now you may not have noticed that there actually is an "ee" sound before the "oo." It may not seem like a very big deal until you say the word "few" without the "ee" sound. Try it. You end up with the word "foo," which is fine if you're describing a kind of Chinese egg dish or a Chinese palace dog. Without the vanishing "ee" at the beginning of the word, the sound of the word "few" is lost.

How Diphthongs Relate to Choral Blend

A lot has been written about choral blend. For me, blend comes down to a very simple statement:

Blend is everyone singing the same vowel, the same way, at the same time.

This is why an understanding of diphthongs is so important to your performance as a choral singer. When a singer "sticks out," it usually has less to do with how loudly they're singing than the tone quality or the "color" of the vowel they're singing. Virtually all problems of choral blend are resolved when every member of the chorus is producing vowels the same way and sustaining the same vowel in a word containing a diphthong.

Now select a piece of music and go through it with a pencil. Find all of the pure vowels, diphthongs, and triphthongs. Sing them as a group, being very careful to sing all of the sustaining vowels exactly together by holding them longer than necessary until every single voice in the group is in total agreement. This is how you blend.

Chapter 7

Consonants

Consonants serve more purpose than simply separating one vowel from another and giving meaning to the sounds you make. I'm going to discuss two other areas in which consonants are helpful and even critical to successful singing. Both have to do with how consonants can help you energize the vowels, which actually carry the singing tone.

Using Consonants as "Starting Blocks"

Think of consonants at the *beginning* of syllables the way you would the starting blocks if you're running a sprint, or the initial charge off the line of scrimmage when the football is snapped. Certain consonants carry great energy with them if you tap into it. Think about the potential energy that is stored behind the lips, teeth, or tongue with consonants like b, the hard c, ch, d, f, the hard g, j (which sometimes can be pronounced almost like ch), k, p, sh, st, t, or v. Using that energy at the beginning of a syllable, especially at the beginning of a word, will energize the vowel that follows as surely as an explosive start out of the blocks or off the line will energize the run that follows. It's virtually impossible to sing an energized, assertive consonant followed by a passive, wimpy vowel. (Well, I suppose it could be done if you really tried, but why would anyone want to?) Learn to use this consonant energy. It will not only energize your vowel production, but will help clarify your enunciation.

57

As a demonstration to yourself, take a piece of music on which you are now working and try to speak the text **without using any vowels.** Put a tremendous amount of energy and force behind the pronunciation of the consonants. Now go back and say the same text with the vowels, but use the same energy on the consonants as you did without the vowels. You will find that as a result of the greater intensity on the consonants, your vowels are now much more energized as well.

Using Consonants as "Follow-through"

Now think of consonants at the end of syllables, especially at the end of words and phrases, as *follow-through*. Follow-through is critical when hitting or throwing a baseball, driving a golf ball, spiking a volleyball, tackling a runner, shooting a basketball, kicking a soccer ball—there are countless examples in sports of how follow-through is critical to success. Now consider what would happen to that particular action if you failed to follow through. Singing an energized, assertive consonant at the end of a syllable, word, or phrase virtually guarantees that the vowel preceding it will also be energized. And there are few things more irritating to choral directors and festival judges than final consonants dropped off the ends of phrases.

Take the same piece of music and make a point of exaggerating the final consonant of each word that ends in a consonant. Especially emphasize the final consonant of the phrase. Again you will discover that the vowel that precedes each consonant energized in such a way will also be energized to a new level.

What Happens When You Don't Have a Consonant?

Frequently, you will have to sing one word that ends with a vowel followed by another word that begins with a vowel. Without a consonant to separate them, the meaning can become a bit cloudy and vague. This is not a problem in Italian where blending one vowel into another is typical of the way the language is spoken. But English is another matter entirely. So what I'm about to tell you right now does not apply to Italian.

Have you ever taken a close look at window paintings in fast-food restaurants? Figures of elves or Easter bunnies or things like that? If you look closely you'll notice that the figures are usually outlined in black. That's because the glass does not provide a background for the figures. So the artist must create the illusion of a background by providing one. This is a little bit like what you have to do in English when separating vowels.

You can create this separation by adding a very soft, gentle glottal stop. Be sure to remember that I said, "very soft, gentle." Doing this too harshly can create a sound that is unpleasant and, in some more extreme cases, it can actually be harmful to your vocal cords. This glottal stop is actually caused by holding the breath momentarily to separate the sound of the two vowels.

By paying closer attention to the way you sing consonants and by applying the energy contained in them, your text will be more easily understood, and your singing will be more energized, exciting, and expressive.

Onomatopoeia—Think "Batman"

One more interesting and fun point about words. Do you know what *onomatopoeia* is? Watch the old *Batman* TV series or movies whenever there's a fight, and you'll see the screen fill up with onomatopoeic words like "Buzz!" "Zap!" "Boom!" We use many words that are onomatopoeic in character, although they're not true onomatopoeia. Say the word "hot." Now say it onomatopoeically. You probably said it with a certain breathiness, almost like a hiss, in your voice. Do the same thing with the word "cold." You probably said it with a very hard "k" sound at the beginning and maybe even a bit of a shiver in your voice. My favorite is the word "greasy." If you say it correctly, you should feel like you need to wash your hands. Your singing will be much more interesting, meaningful, and fun, both for you and your listeners, if you learn to apply what you know about the use of consonants and vowels to this kind of expression of the text.

Chapter 8

Intonation

This is actually my favorite topic because we use the same word *pitch* in both music and baseball. I've heard it said that one of the most difficult things to do in all of sports is to hit a round ball with a round bat squarely. Doesn't make a whole lot of sense when you think about it that way, but that's exactly what the hitter is expected to do. Hitting the pitch squarely means the objective is to hit a line drive, making contact right in the center of the pitch. Theoretically it is possible for a batter never to strike out, but never to hit a pitch cleanly or squarely enough to get a line drive or even a ground ball with enough power to find its way through the infield. If the ball is hit a bit too low, you get a pop-up. A bit too high, you get a weak ground ball. Although such a hitter may never strike out, this would not be considered a very effective hitter.

Singing in tune often is much the same way. Singers will frequently sing the correct pitch, demonstrating they have learned the notes and know the music. But they never really quite hit the pitch squarely in the middle—usually pop-ups and ground balls, rarely line drives. This is every bit as much a matter of mental effort as physical. It has to do with learning and knowing the sound of a melody, even a simple scale, sung precisely in tune, and then producing a pitch that matches it just as precisely. Being close is not good enough. I have a term for notes that are very close but not quite there—*crack notes*. For example, a C-sharp that is sung just a little bit flat but is not flat enough to be called C-natural is C-crack. Take a look at a piano keyboard. You'll see what I mean. It's in there somewhere.

Things You Can Do to Teach Yourself to Sing in Tune

One of the best things you can do for yourself to help you learn to sing in tune is to learn how to play a C-major *diatonic* scale on the piano (all white keys), one hand, one octave, ascending and descending. Learn to play it with correct fingering as long as you're doing it. Starting with the thumb (1) on C, the fingering going up is 1-2-3-1-2-3-4-5.

Many of you probably already know how to do this, so you can teach it to others in the group. Sing with the piano as you play. Use "la-la-la" or "1-2-3" or "do-re-mi." It doesn't really matter—it's just a drill. Then start "covering" the keys—touch each key but only press down and sound every other one, then every third one, then one or two per octave, to "spot" yourself (like someone who acts as a spotter for a weightlifter or gymnast). Do this until you can sing the whole scale precisely in tune, hitting each pitch squarely in the center. No pop-ups, no ground balls, just line drives every time. Think of each step in the scale the way you would steps on a staircase. Each step is (or should be) uniformly the same height from the one before and after it. If the rise is precisely eight inches, you don't get to choose to step up seven-and-a-half inches on one, nine on the next, then eight, then seven-and-a-half again. Sure, that averages out to eight inches, but it doesn't work that way. Each step must land precisely eight inches from the previous step for you to make it safely and successfully to the top. That's how you need to learn to sing your scale.

When you start to get good at the diatonic scale, then learn to play a *chromatic* scale (every key, black and white). Again, learn one octave, one hand, ascending and descending, with correct fingering. If you start on C, the fingering is 1-3-1-3-1-2-3-1-3-1-3-1-2 (thumb is 1). Follow the same procedure until you can sing a chromatic scale, one octave up and down, *precisely.* If you can learn to do this, you're well on your way to hitting line drives every time you sing.

When you've gotten to the point where you can sing these two scales accurately and easily, try a *whole tone scale.* Start on C and play every other key *regardless of color.* That would make the scale C-D-E-F#-G#-A#-C.

Then try mixing whole and half steps in exercises. For instance, try an arpeggio in major going up and minor coming down (C-E-G-C-G-E♭-C) or the other way around (C-Eb-G-C-G-E♮-C).

Or try a scale that alternates whole steps and half steps (C-D-E♭-F-F#-G#-A-B-C). Even if you can only spend five minutes a day working on your intonation in this manner, you will quickly notice a remarkable improvement.

Using Your Breathing Technique to Keep You "Balanced"

Your ability to sing in tune is entirely dependent on your ability to use adequate breath support as discussed in Chapter 3. Can you remember the first time you tried to ride a bicycle without training wheels? In order to keep your balance you probably needed a push to help give you momentum. Without that extra support you were likely to lose your balance at first. After awhile you learned how to ride using your own internal sense of balance, even to the point where you could ride slowly enough to keep pace with someone who is walking beside you, or even stop completely and keep your balance. Although this takes little or no momentum, it still requires a great deal of physical intensity and mental concentration and focus. Think of your breath support as that extra momentum you need to help keep you "balanced," or centered in the middle of the pitch. Right now you need all the breath support you can get. Eventually you will learn how to sing with precise intonation with a minimum of air, but no less physical intensity and mental focus.

Stealing Second Base—Don't Cheat

One tendency singers often have is to "cheat" in the direction of a melody line. Descending passages are especially vulnerable to this problem. If you are singing a downward scale, be sure to land squarely in the middle of each individual note. The same holds true if you are going up to a single note on top and coming right back down. It's like leading off first base with the intention of stealing second against a pitcher with a very good pick-off move. If you cheat or lean back towards first, you'll never get the jump you need to take second. On the other hand, if you cheat or lean towards second and the pitcher comes at you with that great pick-off move, you'll get hung out to dry. So you have to be squarely in a position either to dive back to first safely if the throw comes your way, or break for second when you see the opportunity.

You need to think of music as happening both vertically and horizontally at the same time.

Does anyone remember the Rubik's Cube? The problem is to find a solution in one direction—vertical or horizontal—without creating a problem in the other direction. The challenge is to find a way to coordinate your moves so that you solve problems in both directions simultaneously. Music must be sung with attention focused simultaneously on each note being sung accurately (vertical) while assigning each note its proper place in the context of the musical phrase (horizontal). This is called phrasing. This chapter was about the vertical aspect. The next chapter is about the horizontal one.

Chapter 9

Phrasing

Which usually comes first, the words or the music? If we're talking about popular music of the last fifty or one hundred years, then it can be difficult to tell sometimes, especially with the many singer/songwriters who will say that the words and music come together. But if we're talking about the vast majority of choral music composed over the last six or seven centuries, which is typically what most choral groups perform most of the time, then the question is much easier to answer. Religious music in particular is pretty obvious. Whether we're talking about musical settings of the Latin mass or magnificat, or psalms or other passages from the Bible used for motets or cantatas in Latin or German, it is clear that the text inspired the music. For centuries composers have chosen to enhance poetry in all languages by providing it with a musical setting. Every time you pick up a piece of music, check at the top, usually on the left-hand side, to see if someone other than the musical composer is given credit for writing the text.

Using the Text to Determine Phrasing

What is the single, most obvious difference between vocal music and instrumental music? Singers have words, of course! Instrumentalists have only the music to consider when deciding how to phrase a piece of music. Singers must also consider the words. If we can agree that in a given piece of vocal music, solo or choral, the text came first and, we might assume, it was the inspiration for the music, then it stands to reason that when we interpret that piece we should first give consideration to the textual phrasing before the musical phrasing. Claudio Monteverdi, the great Italian composer whose career bridged the gap between the Renaissance and Baroque eras, recognized the importance of the text in the interpretation of music and put it this way:

**The words, the text, with all its values and qualities,
should be the master and not the servant of
the musical harmony.**

Phrasing is usually, although not exclusively, associated with breathing. The first thing to do with a new piece of music when you are trying to decide where to breathe and how to phrase is simply to speak the text as if it were a piece of poetry or prose. Do this *before* you learn the rhythm of the music, since it gets harder for many people to speak the text of a piece independent of the musical rhythm after they've learned it. Try reciting "Mary Had a Little Lamb" expressively without using the rhythm you normally use when it's sung. Not so easy, is it? It's hard to get the musical rhythm out of your head. Try reciting the Pledge of Allegiance dramatically, without breaking it into the nine or ten fragments like most people do.

The whole point of giving careful consideration to phrasing is to make the text more meaningful and easier to understand for your listeners. The easiest way to phrase a piece of music is by observing the punctuation. There are many exceptions to this rule, such as a dramatic breath in the middle of a phrase at the end of a piece just before you sing a final note that is four measures long. But on the other hand, I have heard singers breathe in the middle of a word for no other reason than it was a convenient place to breathe and they needed the air. That would be like calling time-out just because the pace of the game has slowed for a moment. Time-outs must be very carefully considered if they are to be used most effectively.

I have two very important things to say about breathing at the most appropriate time:

1. Convenience or need for air are NEVER good reasons to take a breath;

2. You must practice your "breathing rhythm" just as much as you must practice singing the correct pitches, rhythms, and words of the music.

What Kind of Breath do You Need to Take?

When you study a phrase to decide where and when you should breathe, you also need to think about the *kind* of breath you are going to take. Do you have lots of time between phrases with a long phrase coming up so you can afford a big, slow, leisurely breath? Do you only have a brief moment to take a short yet full breath? Are you in the middle of a long run in a fugue from a Bach cantata that requires a series of short, quick breaths? You need to make that determination and practice taking the right kind of breath as you learn the piece.

There are, of course, times when a phrase is impossibly long and more air must be taken just to get through it, but that is still never a good reason to take a breath. It's a *reason*, just not a *good* reason. In a choral piece, that's what staggered breathing is for, but even that must be worked out carefully. And in most cases, careful planning and practice will help you avoid breathing in places that detract from the expressiveness of the piece. Just as calling a time-out at the wrong time can interrupt your momentum, so can breathing at the wrong place interrupt the flow and drive of a musical phrase. But just as calling a time-out at the right time can improve your chances of winning for any number of reasons, so can breathing at the right time improve your expressiveness and make your performance more meaningful.

Staggered breathing is really more a matter of knowing two things:

1. When not to breathe, and

2. avoiding getting caught when you do.

Usually there will be one or two critical places in a phrase where breathing would really interrupt its flow. Be sure you know where those places are, and then plan your breath *anywhere* else! When you do "sneak" a breath, be sure to lay off the consonant, because that's the surest giveaway.

Another thing to consider is planning your breathing so that you never completely run out of breath. Have you ever run out of gas in your car? Most of us have, or will, at one time or another. The simple answer to avoiding this little embarrassing event is to refuel before you run out. Never let the tank reach empty.   Plan your breathing when you sing the same way. An-

ticipate what your breath needs are going to be, and always keep some in reserve. If you plan properly, you should never be caught short. It's not like gas stations where you might get caught on the open highway miles away from a pump. Air is all around us, and it's plentiful and free. Take all you need.

Thoughts on "Shaping" the Phrase: Ocean Tides

A phrase is something like an ocean tide. About twice every 24 hours, high tide comes in and reaches its peak. Then each time it flows back out to reach low tide. But each high tide-low tide cycle does not arrive with a steady progression. It is the result of a long series of waves that individually peak and break on the shore, then recede, followed by another wave that peaks and recedes, and so on, until one wave that is the peak has arrived to mark the highest point of high tide or one wave has receded to a point that marks the lowest point of low tide. Now telescope this 12-hour process into a musical phrase of a few measures.

Each phrase has a highest point. It may also have other high points. It also has a lowest point. And there are numerous other notes that are part of the cycle of progression and recession. Each note plays an important part in that cycle.

It is important to remember that:

Every note is important, but all notes are not equal in importance.

The first thing you want to do is find the highest point of a phrase. There are three keys that will help you determine what that high point is:

1. Look for the strongest syllable of the key word, or just the strongest word if it's a single syllable.

2. Look for the highest note in the phrase.

3. Look for the strongest rhythmic beat of the phrase.

Often you get lucky and find all three on a single note/beat/syllable. Frequently you will find two of the three. Every note you sing should either be going toward that high point or going away from it.

Take out a piece you're rehearsing and apply this practice to a few phrases. You'll find there will be some disagreement. That's okay. I frequently disagree with myself, which gets real interesting. But eventually you have to arrive at a decision. Sometimes you may find you have more than one high point. Then it's a matter of assigning relative importance to each note or word in the phrase. Don't labor too meticulously over this process. Just try to find a comfortable flow to the text. Then read it expressively. Then sing it that way. You will enjoy it more, and so will your audience. They may not know why, but you will.

Rests in the Middle of a Phrase: Eagles Flying Behind Trees

One more point about phrasing. Sometimes composers will intentionally put a short rest right in the middle of a lyrical phrase. That does not necessarily mean that a breath should be taken there. In northern Wisconsin we see bald eagles on a fairly regular basis. They are such magnificent birds that people frequently stop whatever else they're doing, even driving, to watch them in flight. If you've followed the flight path of a bird like this, you may lose it momentarily as it goes behind a tree. But your eye still follows its path, anxiously waiting for it to emerge on the other side. Even though you can't see the bird for a moment, **it is still moving forward.** This is how you need to consider musical phrases so that the rest is observed without interrupting the flow of the music.

Remember that when you sing a song, you are really telling a story. All of these recommendations are designed to help you become a better, more interesting, more effective storyteller.

Chapter 10

Recap

This little manual is designed to help you develop your individual skills as a singer. If you were putting together the best choral group that you could, normally you would begin by trying to recruit the best singers available. Then comes the fun part—building a great team with the individual talent you've assembled. If you're already part of a great team, fantastic. But just imagine how great that team will be if each member accepts the challenge and assumes the responsibility of maximizing their talent.

The whole point of all of this discussion about your individual technique and skill as a singer is important only as far as it helps you become a better, more expressive singer. Keep this in mind: **Technique is the servant of expression.** You may have all the greatest ideas in the world of how to express a song, but if you don't have the technique to execute them, they stay hidden in your imagination. You should see all the fantastic moves I can make on a basketball court—in my mind. The technique just isn't there anymore. Okay, most of it never really was. The more technical skill you develop in terms of tone, diction, dynamics, articulation, phrasing, and anything else you can think of, the more expressive and, as a result, entertaining, exciting, and successful a singer you will be.

Keep in mind another important thing. If you were as good right now as you could possibly be, if there was absolutely no more room for growth or improvement, you're still not as good as you'll be a year or two or five from now. You're young. You are years from reaching full physical vocal maturity, from reaching your peak. Check out the notices for auditions for the top opera companies around the country. They have age limits—usually well into the thirties. That means they define 32 or 35 years old, depending on the voice, as a young, promising, developing singer. That's because they know how long it takes for a voice to fully mature and reach its full potential. So you've got lots of time, but don't wait. Get started now. Good luck.

Glossary

Abdominal Cavity: Space below the diaphragm that contains the stomach

Approximate: When the vocal cords come together to phonate

Arytenoids (pronounced ah-RIH-tehn-oid): Cartilages in the larynx that control the movement of the vocal cords

Blend: Everyone singing the same vowel the same way at the same time

Breath Support: The "legs" of your voice

Diaphragm: Muscle membrane that contracts to inhale and divides the thoracic cavity from the abdominal cavity

Diphthongs: Combinations of "pure" vowels that create single-syllable vowels with two vowel sounds

Epiglottis: A tongue-shaped piece of cartilage at the top of the trachea that drops down to seal off the trachea when swallowing

Expiration: Breathing out

Follow-through: Energetic use of consonants at the end of a word or phrase

Glottal stop/glottal attack: Soft, gentle use of closed glottis (holding your breath) to begin a word that begins with a vowel

Glottis: Space between the vocal cords

Inner Ear: Part of your brain that allows you to "hear" a tune without actually hearing it

Inspiration: Inhaling

Intonation: Singing in tune

Laryngeal pharynx (also laryngopharynx): The space in the pharynx immediately above the larynx

Larynx (pronounced LAIR-inks): Voice box, contains the vocal cords (should function like an automatic transmission)

Mucous: Liquid produced by the mucous membranes in the larynx necessary to lubricate

Nasopharynx: The space behind the nose

Onomatopoeia: Naming a thing or action by a vocal imitation of the sound associated with it

Onomatopoeic: Singing a word expressively so its performance sounds like the thing or action the word represents

Oral Cavity: The mouth

Oropharynx: The space immediately behind the mouth, where your tonsils are located

Passagio: The point where the vocal mechanism "shifts" from one register to another; also known as your "break"

Pharynx (pronounced FARE-inks)**:** Passage from the top of the trachea to the area behind the nose

Phonation: Making sound by vibration

Posture: Form your body must assume for best singing production

Projection: The result of good tonal focus, adequate breath support, and release of tension in the vocal mechanism

Raw material: Clear, free, supported, focused tone that provides the basis for beautiful singing

Register: "Gear" in the vocal range, basically the "upper register" and the "lower register"

Resonance: Natural acoustical amplification caused by the vibration of the vocal cords

Resonating Chambers: Laryngeal pharynx, oropharynx, nasopharynx, oral cavity

Staggered Breathing: Individual members of a chorus breathing at different times so that the ensemble can carry a very long phrase without interruption

Starting Blocks: Energetic use of consonants at the beginning of a word or phrase

Tension: The enemy of vocal production

Thoracic Cavity: Space above the diaphragm, within the thorax, that contains the heart and lungs

Thorax: Rib cage

Thyroid Cartilage: Adam's apple

Tone Color: Quality of vowel sound

Trachea: Windpipe

Triphthongs: Combinations of "pure" vowels that create single-syllable vowels with three vowel sounds

Vertical Vowels: Most resonant and spacious vowel sounds based on vertical placement of mouth

Vocal cords: Ligaments inside the larynx that vibrate to phonate

Vocal Instrument: Your whole body

Key phrases to remember (and memorize):

Your breath support is the "legs" of your vocal production.

Nothing you eat or drink has any immediate, direct effect on
your vocal cords.

What is the best possible tone I can produce on any given pitch.

Blend is everyone singing the same vowel the same way
at the same time.

The words, the text, with all its values and qualities, should be the master and not the servant of the musical harmony. —*Claudio Monteverdi*

Every note is important, but all notes are not equal in impotantance.

Technique is the servant of expression.

The Respiratory System

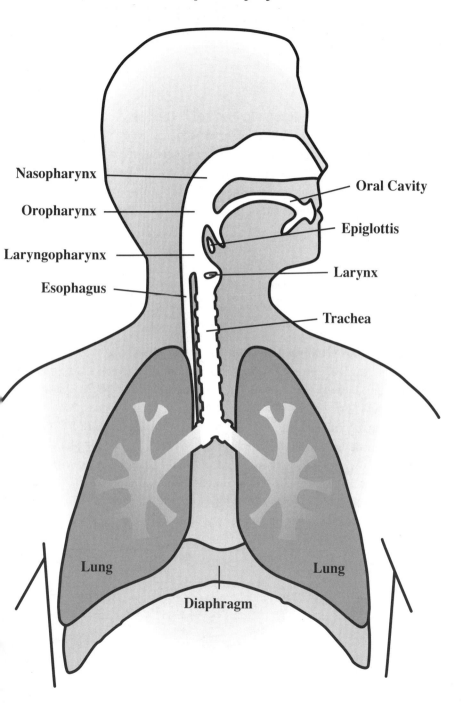

Nasopharynx

Oropharynx

Laryngopharynx

Esophagus

Oral Cavity

Epiglottis

Larynx

Trachea

Lung

Lung

Diaphragm

About the Author

Burbank, California, native **Hank Alviani** holds a BA in Music Education from Mount St. Mary's College in Los Angeles where he studied conducting with Paul Salamunovich. He holds the MM in Choral Conducting from California State University Fullerton where he studied with Howard Swan and John Cooksey, and the DMA from Arizona State University where he was graduate assistant conductor for Douglas McEwen. He also was a Master Class conducting student of Helmuth Rilling at the Oregon Bach Festival. For twelve years he taught junior and senior high school choral music in Southern California, and, since 1993, at the college level in both Texas and Wisconsin.

Currently, Dr. Alviani is Assistant Professor of Music and Director of Choral and Vocal Music Studies at Clarion University of Pennsylvania, a position he has held since 2003. In addition to directing Concert Choir, Madrigal Singers, and Show Choir, he teaches studio voice and voice class, choral conducting, choral methods, and supervises student teachers. He performs regularly with the Pittsburgh Opera Chorus, and is a member of ACDA and MENC. Dr. Alviani is Faculty Advisor for both the Clarion University student chapter of ACDA and Phi Mu Alpha Sinfonia, which awarded him the Orpheus Award in May 2006 for his contributions to music in America.